the LOST ART
of LOGICAL THINKING

KEVIN B DIBACCO

DISCLAIMER

writing. With the ever-changing nature of the subjects included, the author hopes that the reader will be able to appreciate the content that has been covered in this book. While all attempts have been made to verify each piece of information provided in this publication, the author assumes no responsibility for any error, omission, or contrary interpretation of the subject present in this book. Please note that any help or advice given hereof is not a substitution for licensed medical advice. The reader accepts responsibility in the use of any information and takes advice given in this book at their own risk. If the reader is under medication supervision or has had complications with health-related risks, consult your primary care physician as soon as possible before taking any advice given in this book.

"The information and advice contained in this book are based upon the research and the personal and professional experiences of the author. They are not intended as a substitute for consulting with a healthcare professional. The publisher and author are not responsible for any adverse effects or consequences resulting from the use of any of the suggestions, preparations, or procedures discussed in this book. All matters pertaining to your physical health should be supervised by a healthcare professional."

CONTENTS

About the Author   1

CHAPTER 1
Logical thinking overview   4

CHAPTER 2
Introduction to Logical Thinking: What is Logical Thinking?   16

CHAPTER 3
The Fundamental Principles of Logic: Deductive Reasoning   26

CHAPTER 4
Logical Thinking in Business: Applying Logical Thinking to Problem-Solving   39

CHAPTER 5
Enhancing Decision: Making as a Parent with Logical Thinking   48

CHAPTER 6
Logical Thinking for Students: Improving Academic Performance with Logical Thinking   57

CHAPTER 7
Logical Thinking in the Workplace: Using Logical Thinking for Efficient Time Management   66

CHAPTER 8
Logical Thinking for Public Servants: The Role of Logical Thinking in Political Decision-Making   75

CHAPTER 9
Logical Thinking for Athletes: Enhancing Performance through Logical Thinking   85

CHAPTER 10
Overcoming Logical Fallacies: Recognizing and Avoiding Common Logical Fallacies   94

CHAPTER 11
The Power of Logical Thinking in Everyday Life: Applying Logical Thinking to Personal Relationships   103

CHAPTER 12
Harnessing Your Full Logical Thinking Potential: Continuous Improvement and Practice for Logical Thinking   112

CHAPTER 13
Recap of the Power of Logical Thinking   121

ABOUT THE AUTHOR

Kevin understands adversity and the temptation to quit better than most. His life has been a testament to the power of perseverance despite severe hardship. Now, he shares his story and tools to inspire others to get off the mat when knocked down by life.

Kevin's health struggles began early, needing major surgery at just 16 years old. In his 20s and 30s, he endured 6 knee operations, 2 back surgeries, including spinal fusion, 2 hip replacements, and treatment for an aggressive brain tumor. Enduring over 10 major medical procedures would be enough to make anyone feel like giving up. Even as he was writing this, Kevin was struck by Covid-19. As if that weren't another setback, Kevin developed Pneumonia and spent the spring of 2022 and the summer of 2023 having to get daily nebulizer treatments. Once again, his theories were put to the test. Once again, they worked!

Kevin refused to see himself as a victim of circumstance. Through each diagnosis and rehabilitation, he consciously worked to reframe adversity as an opportunity for growth. Instead of sadly ruminating on limitations, he focused positively on each small win — standing, walking, and climbing stairs during recovery. He visualized himself healed and happy against all odds.

Kevin leaned on his deep faith and the support of loved ones during the darkest times. When fear or hopelessness crept in, he prayed for the strength to take the next step forward. He turned to uplifting books and sayings for encouragement. Slowly but surely, he reclaimed his active lifestyle step by step. Through his journey, Kevin realized firsthand the power of mindset to determine one's life experience. He discovered that he could transform his outer reality by controlling his inner world: his thoughts, beliefs, and visualizations. Now, he hopes to share these lessons with others facing major life challenges.

Kevin's book recounts his medical battles, along with the techniques he used to stay grounded in positivity. He provides exercises to overcome negative self-talk, face fears, and visualize desired outcomes. Kevin believes we can all learn to reframe difficulties as growth opportunities. Wherever we feel like quitting, he urges us to proclaim, "I will keep going!"

Kevin's dramatic story provides living proof that, regardless of what knocks us down, we can choose to get back up. We all have access to inner reserves of strength to endure the unendurable. Kevin hopes his book will inspire others to fight major life battles to find their power to keep progressing. By committing to personal growth, we can overcome any obstacle, including those within our minds.

CHAPTER 1

LOGICAL THINKING OVERVIEW

Logical thinking skills are essential for career development as they enable individuals to make informed decisions, generate innovative ideas, set goals, and solve problems. In the job industry, and as you advance in your career, you will encounter numerous challenges that require strong logical reasoning skills for effective problem-solving. Before moving forward and finding solutions, it is crucial to understand what logical thinking entails.

Logical thinking involves disciplined thinking, where significant thoughts are based on evidence and facts. It requires incorporating logic into one's thinking process when analyzing problems and devising solutions.

The importance of logical thinking is underscored by its recognition as one of the top skills employers seek in job candidates, according to a global report. The ability to problem-solve, think critically, and reason logically is highly valued. The significance of logical thinking can be understood through several key points:

- It encourages independent thinking: Independent reasoning abilities are crucial for problem-solving, as extended demonstrations and examples may not always be practical. Logical thinking enables individuals to analyze and reason independently.

- It promotes creativity and innovation: Logical thinking allows individuals to encourage creative thinking and devise creative solutions to issues. It provides a controlled framework for innovation and adds a sense of structure to events in one's life.

- Not only that, but it enhances analytical thinking: Logical reasoning involves weighing different options and evaluating potential outcomes to ensure favorable decisions. It enables individuals to approach multiple-choice questions in various ways, leading to better solutions and outcomes.

- It strengthens the brain: Logical reasoning engages various parts of the brain, such as memory and verbal-logic memory. This process helps strengthen the brain and enhances an individual's ability to discern significant aspects of life.

- It enhances focus: Logical thinking is an effective way to increase concentration and focus. Reasoning ability tests require individuals to focus on problem-solving and employ various methods and strategies, leading to the development of positive self-esteem.

- To improve logical thinking abilities, individuals can engage in activities such as learning from mistakes, anticipating future events, taking complex mental tests, and stimulating the brain. Through various activities, differentiating between observation and inferences, recognizing repetitive patterns, and indulging in analytical values like critical thinking and decision-making.

Logical thinking skills involve focusing on tasks and activities by following a chain of thought processes and relating statements to one another. This enables individuals to find logical solutions to problems.

TO BUILD LOGICAL THINKING SKILLS, INDIVIDUALS CAN CONSIDER THE FOLLOWING TECHNIQUES:

Understanding and considering others' perspectives, devising efficient strategies before starting tasks, analyzing the meaning of words and sentences, and enhancing thinking skills through games and mystery books.

Thinking logically involves rationalizing thoughts and creating positive outcomes. It combines situational awareness, emotional regulation, and efficient decision-making. To think logically, individuals can engage in creative activities, practice asking meaningful questions, spend time with others to gain alternative perspectives, learn new skills frequently, and visualize the outcomes of decisions.

When considering the meaning of logical thinking, it is essential to recognize the emotional reasoning and intelligence involved. Logical thinking involves self-awareness of emotions and preventing them from influencing decision-making processes. Four significant components of logical thinking include deductive reasoning, inductive reasoning, causal inference, and analogy. These components enable individuals to reach specific conclusions, rely on generalizations, recognize change and evolution, and find connections between different perspectives.

Examples of thinking logically in various situations include resolving disagreements, completing pending work before engaging in leisure activities, making tough decisions by considering future opportunities, seeking clarification when unsure, and using logical reasoning to address problems in the workplace.

Logical thinking is the act of analyzing situations, using reasoning abilities to study concerns, and making rational conclusions. It involves gathering information, assessing facts, and methodically making decisions. Logical thinking is a valuable tool for brainstorming ideas, analyzing issues, and finding solutions in various settings, including homes, workplaces, and educational institutions.

FREQUENTLY ASKED QUESTIONS (FAQS):

1. How do you know you are a logical thinker? You can consider yourself a logical thinker if you are attentive, clearly understand facts, and possess clear ideas about situations.
2. Is logical thinking a soft skill? Yes, logical thinking is a soft skill that can be practiced and improved to enhance reasoning abilities.
3. What careers use logical thinking? Numerous careers, such as economists, software developers, accountants, chemical engineers, technical writers, and criminologists, require logical thinking skills.
4. What are logical thinkers good at? Logical thinkers excel at observing and analyzing situations, feedback, and reactions to draw rational conclusions.

LOGICAL THINKING BACKGROUND

Logical thinking refers to the process of using reason and logic to analyze ideas, solve problems, and make decisions. It involves carefully breaking down arguments or situations to evaluate their components in a step-by-step, methodical way. While logical thinking has been practiced throughout history in various forms, several key developments helped establish it as a formal system of thought.

Ancient Greek philosophers like Aristotle developed principles of logic and formalized methods for deductive reasoning. Aristotle's work on syllogisms provided a framework for valid logical argument structure that is still influential today. The medieval logicians later expanded on Aristotle's logic, developing additional rules of inference. In the 17th and 18th centuries, philosophers such as Leibniz, Locke, and Kant explored logical reasoning and its role in knowledge and belief formation.

However, it was in the 19th and 20th centuries that logical thinking was refined into a more rigorous and mathematical system known as symbolic or mathematical logic. Pioneers in this field include George Boole, who devised a system of logical algebra; Gottlob Frege, who formulated predicate logic; and Bertrand Russell and Alfred Whitehead, who introduced modern quantified logic in their Principia Mathematica. The development of computer science and artificial intelligence in the 20th century further advanced the analysis and application of logical reasoning.

LOGICAL THINKING IS IMPORTANT FOR VARIOUS REASONS

It helps improve the clarity and coherence of arguments. Breaking down reasoning into a series of logical steps makes it easier to spot inconsistencies, evaluate premises, and determine the validity of arguments. This can aid fields like philosophy, law, and debate that rely heavily on reasoned discourse.

It enables more systematic and objective analysis. Removing subjectivity and emotional influence through logic helps individuals better assess problems and situations. Logic principles also provide standards to evaluate the strength of different forms of reasoning.

It supports improved decision-making. Logical analysis generates insight that may be overlooked in casual thinking. Identifying key options, weighing evidence, and spotting false assumptions leads to better-informed choices. This applies to business, politics, and everyday decisions.

It boosts problem-solving abilities. Logical thinking provides a structured process to work through difficulties methodically. Breaking an issue down into components allows focusing effort on the most relevant details. Logic helps identify solutions supported by facts and sound inferences.

It lays the groundwork for science and mathematics. Formal logic underpins fields like computer science and statistics that rely heavily on precise, mathematical reasoning. The deductive process drives proofs in mathematics and the testing process in science.

It facilitates better learning and educational outcomes. Logical thinking abilities strongly influence how well students acquire and apply knowledge across disciplines. Education systems worldwide recognize logical reasoning as a foundational skill to develop.

While humans are capable of logical thinking from a young age, it is a skill requiring practice and instruction. Methods like the trivium, an ancient framework covering logic, grammar, and rhetoric, provide systematic approaches to cultivating reason. Logic and critical thinking are now common course topics at all levels of education. Standardized tests also frequently access logical thinking abilities.

Professionals in fields like law, science, engineering, accounting, and analytics apply logical thinking habits and formal logic principles regularly in their work. Any complex intellectual job requires evaluating arguments, assessing evidence, analyzing data, and making sound inferences. However, logical reasoning is a useful skill for any career path involving problem-solving, writing, public speaking, or debating. It can also aid everyday decision-making in people's personal lives.

Logical thinking does have limitations. Over-reliance on pure logic detached from emotions, ethics, or subjective experience can lead to conclusions that fail to account for the nuanced complexities of human life. Integrating logical analysis with compassion and diversity of thought is important for fully addressing many issues. Logic also cannot replace creativity and inspiration, which remain essential to humanity's greatest achievements.

Logical thinking refers to the process of using reason methodically to assess ideas and reach supportable conclusions. This mode of thought has been valued since ancient times for strengthening arguments, enhancing analysis, aiding problem-solving and improving decisions. While not perfect, logical reasoning represents an indispensable tool for expanding knowledge, facilitating intellectual discourse, and guiding considered action. Its influence permeates philosophy, science, academia, business, law, and modern intellectual culture. With practice, logical thinking is a skill anyone can cultivate to improve their thinking and approach to life.

CHAPTER 2

INTRODUCTION TO LOGICAL THINKING: WHAT IS LOGICAL THINKING?

In our world, the ability to think logically has become increasingly indispensable. Logical thinking is a fundamental cognitive skill that allows us to reason, analyze, and make sound judgments based on evidence and facts. It is a powerful tool that can unlock our full potential and help us navigate through the complexities of life. Logical thinking can greatly benefit you in your respective field.

So, what exactly is logical thinking? At its core, it is the process of using rational and systematic methods to arrive at conclusions or solutions. It involves breaking down complex problems into smaller, more manageable parts, identifying patterns and relationships, and drawing logical inferences. Logical thinking requires objectivity, accuracy, and a willingness to challenge assumptions and biases.

For businessmen/women, logical thinking is crucial for decision-making. It allows you to evaluate different options, consider the potential risks and rewards, and make sound business choices. By applying logical thinking, you can assess market trends, analyze financial data, and devise effective strategies that drive success and growth.

Mothers can also benefit from logical thinking in their daily lives. From managing household budgets to solving parenting challenges, logical thinking helps prioritize tasks, organize schedules, and find creative solutions. By approaching situations logically, Mothers can make informed decisions and create a harmonious family environment.

Students can enhance their learning experience through logical thinking. It aids in understanding complex concepts, solving mathematical problems, and critically evaluating information. Logical thinking fosters intellectual curiosity, encourages independent thinking, and promotes a more in-depth understanding of various subjects.

In the workplace, logical thinking is a valued skill for workers across all industries. It enables employees to analyze data, identify trends, and solve complex problems efficiently. Logical thinkers are often sought after for their ability to tackle challenges head-on, explore unconventional solutions, and make informed decisions.

Public servants and athletes can also benefit from logical thinking. It helps Public servants analyze policies, develop well-structured arguments, and make rational decisions that benefit their constituents. For athletes, logical thinking aids in strategic planning, assessing opponents' weaknesses, and adapting game plans accordingly.

Logical thinking is a vital skill that transcends different professions and life roles. By honing this cognitive ability, we can unlock our full potential and overcome the challenges that come our way. Embracing logical thinking will empower you to make better decisions, solve problems effectively, and achieve success in your chosen endeavors.

THE IMPORTANCE OF LOGICAL THINKING IN DIFFERENT AREAS OF LIFE

Logic is a powerful tool that plays a crucial role in every aspect of our lives. Whether you are a businessman/woman, a mom, a student, a worker, a politician, or an athlete, logical thinking is essential for success and personal growth. In this chapter, we will explore the significance of logical thinking in various areas of life and how it can help you unlock your full potential. In the business world, logical thinking enables you to make informed decisions based on evidence and reason. It allows you to analyze data, identify patterns, and draw logical conclusions. By employing logical thinking in your business strategies, you can anticipate potential risks, devise effective problem-solving methods, and ultimately drive your organization towards success.

For Mothers, logical thinking helps in managing household tasks, making important decisions, and raising children. It allows you to prioritize tasks, plan routines, and solve problems efficiently. By applying logical thinking, you can teach your children critical thinking skills, empower them to make sound decisions, and foster their problem-solving abilities.

Students greatly benefit from logical thinking as it enhances their learning capabilities. It enables them to comprehend complex concepts, solve mathematical problems, and analyze information critically. By developing logical thinking skills, students can excel in their academic pursuits, become independent learners, and pursue their career goals with confidence.

Workers in various fields can leverage logical thinking to improve their productivity and problem-solving abilities. It enables them to streamline their workflows, identify errors, and develop innovative solutions. By applying logical thinking, workers can enhance their performance, contribute to a more efficient workplace, and advance in their careers.

Public servants rely on logical thinking to understand complex societal issues, analyze policies, and make informed decisions that benefit their constituents. By employing logical thinking, public servants can develop effective strategies, address public concerns, and work towards the betterment of society.

Athletes can also benefit from logical thinking as it helps them strategize their game plans, analyze their opponents' tactics, and make split-second decisions on the field. By using logical thinking, athletes can improve their performance, adapt to changing game situations, and elevate themselves to new heights of success.

Logical thinking is a fundamental skill that is indispensable in every area of life. Whether you are a businessperson, a mom, a student, a worker, a politician, or an athlete, logical thinking empowers you to make informed decisions, solve problems effectively, and achieve your goals. By embracing the power of logical thinking, you can unlock your full potential and pave the way for a successful and fulfilling life.

THE BENEFITS OF DEVELOPING LOGICAL THINKING SKILLS INTRODUCTION

In today's world, the ability to think logically has become an invaluable asset. Whether you are a businessman/woman, a mom, a student, a worker, a politician, or an athlete, honing your logical thinking skills can unlock your full potential and open countless doors of opportunity. In this subchapter, we will explore the numerous benefits of developing logical thinking skills and how it can positively impact different aspects of your life.

1. **Enhanced Problem-Solving Abilities:** Logical thinking equips individuals with the ability to analyze complex problems, break them down into manageable components, and devise effective solutions. By developing this skill, you can tackle challenges with clarity and efficiency, finding innovative solutions that others may overlook. This advantage can greatly benefit businessmen/women, students, workers, and public servants who face daily problem-solving tasks.

2. **Improved Decision-Making:** Logical thinking enables individuals to evaluate different options, weigh their pros and cons, and make informed decisions based on evidence and facts. By cultivating this skill, you can minimize impulsive choices and ensure that your decisions align with your long-term goals. This benefit is crucial for businessmen/women, Mothers, Public servants, and athletes who often face high-pressure situations that require sound judgment.

3. **Heightened Analytical Skills:** Logical thinking involves the ability to critically analyze information, identify patterns, and draw logical conclusions. By developing these analytical skills, individuals can better comprehend complex ideas, detect underlying biases, and make well-reasoned arguments. This advantage is beneficial for students, workers, public servants, and anyone involved in research or data analysis.

4. **Effective Communication:** Logical thinking fosters clear and concise communication. It

allows individuals to organize their thoughts logically, present ideas intelligently and articulate complex concepts effectively. Whether you are negotiating with clients, presenting ideas to stakeholders, or discussing important matters with colleagues, strong logical thinking skills will enhance your ability to convey information persuasively.

Contrary to popular belief, logical thinking and creativity are not mutually exclusive. In fact, logical thinking can fuel creativity by providing a structured framework for generating and evaluating ideas. By developing logical thinking skills, individuals can embrace innovative approaches, challenge assumptions, and approach problems from innovative angles. This advantage is relevant for businessmen/women, students, workers, and athletes who strive for originality and innovation in their respective fields.

The benefits of developing logical thinking skills are pervasive and applicable to various aspects of life. Whether you are a businessman/woman seeking to gain a competitive edge, a mom managing household responsibilities, a student aiming for academic success, a worker navigating a challenging profession, a politician making critical decisions, or an athlete striving for excellence. The power of logical thinking can unlock your full potential, enabling you to thrive in your chosen path. Embrace logical thinking today and witness the transformative impact it can have on your personal and professional life.

CHAPTER 3

THE FUNDAMENTAL PRINCIPLES OF LOGIC: DEDUCTIVE REASONING

In the realm of logical thinking, one powerful tool stands out: deductive reasoning. This method of thought allows us to draw logical conclusions based on a set of premises or statements, guiding us towards sound decisions and efficient problem-solving. Whether you are a businessman/woman, a mom, a student, a worker, a politician, or an athlete, mastering deductive reasoning can unlock your full potential in various aspects of life.

At its core, deductive reasoning involves moving from general statements to specific conclusions. This process is often referred to as "top-down" reasoning, as it starts with broad principles and narrows down to precise outcomes. By utilizing deductive reasoning, individuals can dissect complex situations and unravel intricate problems, ultimately leading to informed judgments.

For businessmen/women, deductive reasoning is an invaluable asset in making strategic decisions. By analyzing market trends, consumer behavior, and financial data, entrepreneurs can deduce patterns and probabilities, thereby increasing the likelihood of success. Deductive reasoning enables them to identify potential risks and rewards, helping them navigate the competitive landscape with confidence and precision.

Mothers, too, can benefit from deductive reasoning in their daily lives. Whether it's managing household chores, organizing schedules, or addressing parenting challenges, applying deductive reasoning allows Mothers to prioritize tasks and make informed choices. By recognizing cause-and-effect relationships and drawing logical conclusions, Mothers can create harmonious environments for their families while optimizing their time and resources.

Students can enhance their academic performance by developing their deductive reasoning skills. From math and science to literature and history, deductive reasoning aids in comprehending complex concepts, solving intricate problems, and constructing well-reasoned arguments. By employing deductive reasoning, students can excel in exams, engage in critical thinking, and acquire a solid foundation for lifelong learning.

Workers across various industries can also leverage deductive reasoning to enhance their problem-solving abilities. Whether you are an engineer, a doctor, a lawyer, or a designer, deductive reasoning helps identify the root causes of issues and develop effective solutions. By logically analyzing data, evaluating options, and predicting outcomes, workers can streamline processes, improve efficiency, and deliver exceptional results.

Public servants and athletes alike can harness the power of deductive reasoning to excel in their respective fields. Public servants can utilize deductive reasoning to analyze policies, predict public reactions, and craft persuasive arguments. Athletes can benefit from deductive reasoning by evaluating opponents' strategies, identifying weaknesses, and devising winning game plans.

Deductive reasoning is a fundamental aspect of logical thinking that holds immense potential for individuals in various walks of life. By mastering this powerful tool, businessmen/women, Mothers, students, workers, public servants, and athletes can unlock their full potential and achieve success in their chosen endeavors. So, let us embrace deductive reasoning and open the door to logical thinking, propelling us towards a brighter, more efficient future.

INDUCTIVE REASONING

In the realm of logical thinking, one of the most powerful tools at our disposal is inductive reasoning. Inductive reasoning allows us to make generalizations and draw conclusions based on specific observations or evidence. It is a fundamental skill that can be applied to various aspects of life, making it invaluable for businessmen/women, Mothers, students, workers, public servants, athletes, and anyone interested in honing their logical thinking abilities.

Inductive reasoning involves moving from specific instances to broader generalizations. It is the process of collecting data, analyzing patterns, and drawing conclusions based on the evidence at hand. This type of reasoning is widely used in scientific research, market analysis, problem-solving, and decision-making.

In business, inductive reasoning can be the key to unlocking new opportunities and gaining a competitive edge. Business professionals can make informed predictions and adapt their strategies by carefully observing consumer behavior, market trends, and industry patterns. Inductive reasoning can also help identify emerging markets and untapped potential, enabling entrepreneurs to seize valuable opportunities.

Mothers, too, can benefit from inductive reasoning in their everyday lives. Mothers can make educated decisions regarding their well-being by paying attention to their children's behavior, habits, and preferences. Whether it's planning nutritious meals, organizing schedules, or addressing emotional needs, inductive reasoning can enable Mothers to provide the best care for their children.

Through inductive reasoning, students and workers can also enhance their learning and problem-solving abilities. They can grasp complex concepts more effectively by analyzing patterns and drawing conclusions from specific examples. Inductive reasoning can help them identify gaps in their knowledge, enabling them to fill those gaps and improve their overall performance.

Public servants and athletes can utilize inductive reasoning to gain insights into their respective fields. Public servants can analyze voting patterns, public opinion, and historical data to formulate better policies and strategies. Athletes can study opponents' tactics, game statistics, and performance trends to devise winning strategies and strengthen their skills.

Inductive reasoning is an essential skill for individuals in various walks of life. It empowers businessmen/women, Mothers, students, workers, public servants, athletes, and anyone interested in logical thinking to make informed decisions, solve problems effectively, and unlock their full potential. By harnessing the power of inductive reasoning, individuals can navigate the complexities of life with greater clarity and achieve success in their chosen endeavors.

CRITICAL THINKING

Today the ability to think critically has become more important than ever. Whether you are a businessman/woman, a mom, a student, a worker, a politician, or an athlete, honing your critical thinking skills is key to unlocking your full potential. This subchapter explores the power of logical thinking and provides practical strategies to enhance your critical thinking abilities.

Critical thinking is the process of objectively analyzing and evaluating information to make informed decisions and solve problems. It goes beyond mere intuition or gut feeling and relies on logic and reasoning. In a world filled with misinformation and biased narratives, the ability to think critically is a valuable asset.

For businessmen/women, critical thinking is crucial in making strategic decisions that can have a significant impact on their organizations. By using logical thinking, they can analyze market trends, assess risks, and develop innovative solutions that give them a competitive edge.

For Mothers, critical thinking helps in making informed decisions about their children's education, health, and overall well-being. Mothers can make choices that positively impact their children's lives by critically evaluating various options and considering different perspectives.

For students, critical thinking is essential for academic success. It allows them to analyze complex texts, evaluate evidence, and construct logical arguments. Students become better equipped to navigate their educational journey and excel in their chosen fields by developing critical thinking skills.

For workers, critical thinking improves problem-solving abilities, fosters creativity, and enhances decision-making skills. It enables them to adapt to changing workplace dynamics, identify opportunities, and contribute meaningfully to their organizations.

For Public servants, critical thinking is vital in analyzing complex policy issues, understanding constituents' needs, and making informed decisions that benefit society as a whole. By applying logical thinking, public servants can develop effective policies and navigate the intricacies of public service.

For athletes, critical thinking helps in strategizing, analyzing opponents' moves, and making split-second decisions during competitions. By employing logical thinking, athletes can identify weaknesses in their opponents and exploit them to achieve victory.

In this subchapter, we will delve into various aspects of critical thinking, including logical reasoning, evaluating evidence, avoiding cognitive biases, and problem-solving techniques. By developing these skills, you will be equipped to face challenges with confidence, make sound judgments, and unlock your full potential. Remember, the power of logical thinking lies within each of us, waiting to be tapped into. By embracing critical thinking, you can enhance your decision-making abilities and become a more effective problem solver in all aspects of your life.

ANALYTICAL THINKING: UNLEASHING THE POWER OF LOGIC IN YOUR LIFE

In a world that is constantly bombarding us with information, the ability to think critically and analytically has become more important than ever. The power of analytical thinking can unlock your full potential and give you a competitive edge in any field.

Analytical thinking is the process of breaking down complex issues or situations into their individual components, examining them critically, and drawing logical conclusions based on evidence and reasoning. It goes beyond surface-level understanding and allows you to delve deep into the heart of any matter, making informed decisions and solving concerns effectively.

For businessmen/women, analytical thinking is essential for strategic planning, risk assessment, and problem-solving. You can identify opportunities and make informed decisions that drive your business forward by critically analyzing market trends, consumer behavior, and financial data. Analytical thinking helps you identify potential risks and devise contingency plans, ensuring the long-term stability of your organization.

Mothers, too, can benefit greatly from analytical thinking. From managing household budgets to making important decisions about their children's education, Mothers are constantly faced with complex situations that require critical analysis. By applying analytical thinking, Mothers can evaluate various options, consider the pros and cons, and make well-informed choices that positively impact their families.

Students can enhance their academic performance through analytical thinking. Students can better understand complex concepts, identify key ideas, and develop logical arguments by critically analyzing information. Analytical thinking also enables students to evaluate different perspectives, challenge assumptions, and think creatively, leading to innovative solutions and improved problem-solving skills.

Analytical thinking is equally crucial for workers in any profession. It enables individuals to identify inefficiencies, streamline processes, and make evidence-based recommendations for improvement. By analyzing data, workers can identify patterns and trends, enabling them to make data-driven decisions that optimize outcomes and drive success.

Public servants and athletes can also benefit from analytical thinking. Public servants can critically analyze policies, evaluate their impact, and make informed decisions that benefit their constituents. Athletes can analyze their opponents' strategies, identify weaknesses, and devise winning game plans.

Analytical thinking is a powerful tool that can revolutionize the way you approach challenges and make decisions in any aspect of your life. By developing your analytical thinking skills, you can unlock your full potential and gain a competitive advantage in today's complex world. So, embrace the power of logic and let analytical thinking propel you towards success.

CHAPTER 4
LOGICAL THINKING IN BUSINESS: APPLYING LOGICAL THINKING TO PROBLEM-SOLVING

Problem-solving skills have become a highly sought-after trait. Whether you are a businessman/woman, a mom, a student, a worker, a politician, or an athlete, the ability to approach problems with logical thinking is essential for success in any field. This subchapter will explore the power of logical thinking and how you can unlock your full potential by applying it to problem-solving.

Logical thinking is a systematic approach to analyzing and evaluating information to reach a sound conclusion or make an informed decision. It involves breaking down complex concerns into smaller, more manageable parts, and then assessing each part individually. We can identify patterns, uncover hidden connections, and make informed judgments by applying logical reasoning.

Businessmen/women can benefit greatly from logical thinking when faced with strategic planning, market analysis, or decision-making challenges. By carefully analyzing data, considering all possible outcomes, and weighing the pros and cons, logical thinking can help them make informed decisions that drive their businesses forward.

Mothers, too, can apply logical thinking to solve everyday problems. Whether it's managing household chores, juggling schedules, or resolving conflicts, logical thinking can help them identify underlying causes, consider multiple perspectives, and find practical solutions that benefit the whole family.

Students can enhance their academic performance by applying logical thinking to problem-solving. Whether it's solving math equations, understanding complex theories, or writing persuasive essays, logical thinking enables them to approach challenges systematically, break down complex concepts into manageable parts, and develop logical arguments.

Workers from various fields can benefit from logical thinking to improve their problem-solving abilities. Whether it's troubleshooting technical difficulties, resolving conflicts among team members, or optimizing processes, logical thinking can help them identify the root cause of problems, analyze available options, and make data-driven decisions.

Public servants can use logical thinking to address societal issues, evaluate policy alternatives, and make informed decisions that benefit their constituents. By carefully considering the evidence, examining the consequences of different actions, and weighing the interests of various stakeholders, logical thinking can guide them in making well-reasoned choices.

Athletes can apply logical thinking to improve their performance and overcome challenges. By analyzing their strengths and weaknesses, identifying areas for improvement, and developing a systematic training plan, logical thinking can help them achieve their goals and excel in their respective sports.

Logical thinking is a powerful tool that can be applied to problem-solving across various domains. By breaking down complex difficulties, considering multiple perspectives, analyzing data, and making informed judgments, individuals from all walks of life can unlock their full potential and achieve success in their respective fields.

MAKING INFORMED DECISIONS WITH LOGICAL THINKING

Making informed decisions is crucial for success in any field. The ability to think logically and make sound judgments is a valuable skill. This subchapter will delve into the power of logical thinking and how it can help you unlock your full potential.

Logical thinking is a systematic approach to problem-solving that involves evaluating facts, evidence, and reasoning to arrive at a rational conclusion. It enables individuals to analyze complex situations, weigh options, and make informed choices. In a world filled with information overload, logical thinking serves as a compass, guiding you towards sound decisions.

For businessmen/women, logical thinking is essential for strategic planning and risk assessment. By considering various factors, such as market trends, financial data, and customer preferences, logical thinkers can identify opportunities and make informed business decisions. It helps them avoid impulsive choices and navigate uncertainties with confidence.

Mothers, too, can benefit from logical thinking in managing their households and raising children. They can prioritize tasks, set realistic goals, and find creative solutions to everyday challenges by applying logical reasoning. Logical thinking empowers Mothers to make informed choices that positively impact their families' well-being and personal growth.

Students can enhance their academic performance by embracing logical thinking. It aids in critical thinking, problem-solving, and effective studying.

Students can excel in exams by analyzing information, recognizing patterns, and drawing logical conclusions and develop a more in-depth understanding of subjects across disciplines.

Workers in any profession can make significant strides by adopting logical thinking. From troubleshooting technical difficulties to resolving conflicts, logical thinkers are equipped to tackle complex problems efficiently. This skill enables workers to streamline processes, improve productivity, and contribute effectively to their organizations.

Public servants and athletes can also benefit from logical thinking in their respective fields. By analyzing data, anticipating outcomes, and evaluating potential risks, they can make sound decisions that have significant impacts on their careers and the lives of others. Logical thinking helps them weigh the pros and cons of different strategies and make informed choices that align with their goals.

Logical thinking is a powerful tool that can unlock your full potential in any area of life. By honing this skill, you can make informed decisions, solve problems, and achieve success. Embracing logical thinking will empower you to navigate challenges, seize opportunities, and thrive in your chosen field.

USING LOGICAL THINKING FOR EFFECTIVE COMMUNICATION IN THE WORKPLACE

Effective communication is more crucial than ever in today's fast-paced and competitive business environment. Whether you are a businessman/woman, a mom, a student, a worker, a politician, or an athlete, the ability to communicate logically and effectively can greatly impact your success. This subchapter will explore the power of logical thinking and how it can enhance your communication skills in the workplace.

Logical thinking is the process of reasoning based on valid and sound arguments. It involves analyzing facts, identifying patterns, and drawing logical conclusions. By adopting this approach, you can communicate your ideas, opinions, and perspectives in a clear, concise, and convincing manner.

One of the key benefits of using logical thinking in communication is that it helps you organize your thoughts. When you approach a topic or problem logically, you break it down into smaller components and evaluate each one separately. This allows you to present your ideas in a structured and coherent manner, making it easier for your audience to understand and engage with your message.

Logical thinking also enables you to anticipate and address potential counterarguments. By considering different viewpoints and potential objections, you can preemptively address them in your communication. This helps you build stronger arguments and increases the likelihood of your message being received positively.

Logical thinking fosters critical thinking skills, which are essential in the workplace. It helps you evaluate information objectively, identify flaws in arguments, and make informed decisions. By applying logical thinking to your communication, you can present well-reasoned and evidence-based arguments that are more likely to persuade others.

In reality, logical thinking promotes problem-solving abilities. It allows you to break down complex problems into manageable parts, analyze them systematically, and identify the most effective solutions. By incorporating logical thinking into your communication, you can articulate your problem-solving process, making it easier for others to understand and collaborate with you.

Logical thinking is a powerful tool that can greatly enhance your communication skills in the workplace. By adopting a logical approach, you can organize your thoughts, address counterarguments, foster critical thinking, and promote problem-solving abilities. Incorporating logical thinking into your communication can unlock your full potential and lead to greater success in your professional and personal life.

CHAPTER 5

ENHANCING DECISION: MAKING AS A PARENT WITH LOGICAL THINKING

As parents, we are constantly faced with making decisions that will shape our children's lives. Whether it's choosing the right school, setting boundaries, or instilling values, these choices can profoundly impact their future. To make the best decisions for our children, it is essential to employ logical thinking.

Logical thinking is a powerful tool that can help us navigate through the complexities of parenthood. It enables us to approach situations with clarity, reason, and objectivity, ultimately leading to better decision-making. By incorporating logical thinking into our parenting practices, we can ensure that our choices are well-informed and aligned with our children's best interests.

One of the key aspects of logical thinking is the ability to analyze information critically. As parents, we are bombarded with an overwhelming amount of advice, opinions, and information. Logical thinking allows us to sift through this sea of information and identify what is relevant and reliable. By evaluating the evidence and considering the potential consequences, we can make decisions that are grounded in reason and logic.

Additionally, logical thinking helps us to identify and challenge our biases and assumptions. As parents, we often have preconceived notions about what is best for our children. These biases can cloud our judgment and hinder us from making rational decisions. By actively questioning our beliefs and seeking alternative perspectives, we can ensure that our decisions are not driven solely by personal biases, but rather by what is truly in the best interest of our children. Another important aspect of logical thinking is the ability to consider multiple solutions and outcomes. By adopting a mindset of flexibility and openness, we can explore different options and anticipate potential consequences. This allows us to make decisions that are based on a comprehensive understanding of the situation, rather than relying on a narrow and limited perspective.

Enhancing decision-making as a parent with logical thinking is a valuable skill that can greatly benefit our children. By employing logical thinking, we can navigate the challenges of parenthood with clarity, reason, and objectivity. This approach enables us to make well-informed decisions that are grounded in evidence, challenge biases, and consider multiple perspectives. As businessmen/women, Mothers, students, workers, public servants, athletes, and individuals interested in logic and logical thinking. Incorporating logical thinking into our parenting practices will empower us to unlock our full potential as parents and ensure the best possible outcomes for our children.

TEACHING LOGICAL THINKING SKILLS TO CHILDREN

Logical thinking skills are crucial for success in various aspects of life. Whether you are a businessman/woman, a mom, a student, a worker, a politician, or an athlete, the ability to think logically can greatly enhance your decision-making abilities and problem-solving skills. This subchapter aims to explore the importance of teaching logical thinking skills to children and the various strategies that can be employed to nurture this vital skill.

Logic and logical thinking are foundational skills that lay the groundwork for a child's cognitive development. By encouraging children to think logically from an early age, we empower them to analyze situations critically, make informed choices, and approach challenges with a structured mindset. Logical thinking enables children to understand cause and effect relationships, identify patterns, and draw logical conclusions.

Parents, educators, and mentors play a significant role in fostering logical thinking skills in children.

One effective strategy is to encourage children to engage in activities that stimulate their logical reasoning abilities. Puzzles, riddles, and brainteasers are excellent tools to develop critical thinking and problem-solving skills. Additionally, introducing children to mathematical concepts from an early age, such as basic operations, algebra, and geometry, can enhance their logical thinking abilities.

Another approach is to incorporate logical thinking into everyday activities. Encourage children to think through their actions and consider the consequences of making decisions. Help them understand the importance of evidence and reasoning in forming opinions and making judgments. Engaging in debates and discussions can also sharpen their logical thinking and communication skills.

Technology can be harnessed to teach logical thinking skills. Educational software and online platforms provide interactive games and exercises that challenge children to think logically and solve problems. Virtual coding classes are also gaining popularity as they introduce children to the logical thinking required for programming.

Teaching logical thinking skills to children is crucial for their overall cognitive development. By instilling logical thinking abilities, we equip them with the tools to navigate complex situations, make sound decisions, and excel in various areas of life. Whether you are a businessman/woman, a mom, a student, a worker, a politician, or an athlete, the power of logical thinking can unlock your full potential.

BALANCING EMOTIONAL AND LOGICAL THINKING IN PARENTING

In the realm of parenting, the delicate balance between emotional and logical thinking is crucial. As businessmen/women, Mothers, students, workers, public servants, athletes, and individuals from various niches, we often find ourselves facing the challenge of managing our emotions while making rational decisions.

This "The Power of Logical Thinking: Unlock Your Full Potential" aims to provide insights and strategies to help you strike that equilibrium. Emotional thinking is an innate aspect of human nature, often driven by our instincts and feelings. It allows us to empathize, connect, and understand others on a deep level. However, when it comes to parenting, relying solely on emotions can sometimes cloud our judgment and hinder effective decision-making. On the other hand, logical thinking provides a rational and objective perspective, enabling us to analyze situations critically and make informed choices.

One of the key aspects of balancing emotional and logical thinking in parenting is understanding the importance of both. Emotional intelligence allows us to connect with our children and respond to their needs, fostering a healthy and nurturing environment. Simultaneously, logical thinking equips us with the ability to set boundaries, establish rules, and make tough decisions for their long-term well-being.

To strike this balance effectively, it is essential to recognize and manage our emotions. As parents, we must cultivate self-awareness, understanding our triggers and biases that may interfere with logical decision-making. By acknowledging and regulating our emotions, we can better respond to our children's needs without compromising their overall development.

Incorporating logical thinking into our parenting approach involves setting clear expectations and boundaries. While emotions might push us to be lenient or overprotective, logical thinking helps us consider the consequences of our actions and make decisions that promote growth and independence in our children.

The subchapter will delve into various strategies and techniques to help businessmen/women, Mothers, students, workers, public servants, and athletes strike the right balance between emotional and logical thinking in their parenting journey. It will explore real-life scenarios and provide practical tips on fostering emotional connection while maintaining logical boundaries. Through this exploration, readers will gain a more profound understanding of how to leverage both emotional and logical thinking to become more effective parents, capable of nurturing their children's emotional well-being while preparing them for the challenges of the world.

CHAPTER 6

LOGICAL THINKING FOR STUDENTS: IMPROVING ACADEMIC PERFORMANCE WITH LOGICAL THINKING

Logical thinking is an essential skill that can greatly enhance academic performance across various fields and disciplines. Whether you are a student, a professional, a parent, or an athlete, the power of logical thinking can unlock your full potential and help you excel in your endeavors.

For students, logical thinking skills are crucial in problem-solving, critical analysis, and decision-making. By honing these skills, students can approach complex subjects with clarity and confidence. Logical thinking allows students to break down complex concepts into manageable components, enabling a more profound understanding of the subject. It also helps students in organizing their thoughts, making connections between different ideas, and identifying patterns and relationships.

Businessmen/women can greatly benefit from logical thinking as well. In a fast-paced and ever-evolving business environment, the ability to think logically allows professionals to make sound decisions, evaluate risks, and identify opportunities. Logical thinking helps in analyzing data, identifying trends, and formulating effective strategies. By applying logical thinking skills, businessmen/women can enhance their problem-solving abilities, expand their communication skills, and foster innovation within their organizations.

Logical thinking is not limited to students and professionals; it is equally important for parents, workers, public servants, and athletes. Parents can use logical thinking to solve family issues, make informed decisions regarding their children's education, and instill critical thinking skills in their kids. Workers can apply logical thinking to improve their productivity, solve workplace problems, and enhance their overall job performance. Public servants can use logical thinking to analyze policy issues, evaluate potential consequences, and make informed decisions for the betterment of society. Athletes can benefit from logical thinking by strategizing their moves, analyzing their opponents' strengths and weaknesses, and making split-second decisions during competitions.

The power of logical thinking lies in its ability to enhance cognitive skills, improve problem-solving abilities, and foster rational decision-making. By developing logical thinking skills, individuals from all walks of life can unlock their full potential and achieve academic excellence. Whether you are a student, a businessman/woman, a parent, a worker, a politician, or an athlete, embracing logical thinking will undoubtedly lead to improved academic performance and success in your chosen field.

STRATEGIES FOR EFFECTIVE STUDYING USING LOGICAL THINKING

Logical thinking is a powerful tool that can be applied to various aspects of life, including studying. Whether you are a student preparing for exams, a working professional seeking to enhance your skills, or a businessman/woman investigating how to improve your decision-making abilities, incorporating logical thinking into your study routine can significantly boost your learning outcomes. In this subchapter, we will explore effective strategies for studying using logical thinking, applicable to a wide range of audiences, including businessmen/women, Mothers, students, workers, public servants, and athletes.

1. **Develop a Structured Approach:** Logical thinking thrives in an organized and structured environment. Start by creating a study plan that outlines specific goals, timeframes, and tasks. Break down complex subjects into smaller, manageable chunks to enhance comprehension and retention.

2. **Analyze Information:** Instead of passively reading or memorizing facts, adopt an analytical approach to studying. Ask critical questions, evaluate evidence, and seek to understand the underlying principles. Challenge assumptions and identify any logical fallacies within the material.

3. **Practice Problem-Solving:** Logical thinking is closely linked to problem-solving abilities. Engage in exercises or case studies that require you to apply logical reasoning to find solutions. This active learning approach reinforces your understanding and helps develop your critical thinking skills.

4. **Make Connections:** Logical thinking thrives on connections and relationships. Seek to establish connections between different concepts, theories, or ideas. Relate new information to existing knowledge or experiences, enabling you to grasp complex subjects more effectively.

5. **Seek Clarity:** Logical thinking demands clarity and precision. Avoid vague or ambiguous

language when studying. Take the time to define key terms, concepts, or definitions to ensure a clear understanding. Use logical frameworks such as mind maps or diagrams to visually represent relationships between ideas.

6. **Evaluate Arguments:** Logical thinking involves the ability to assess the strength and validity of arguments. Practice analyzing and evaluating arguments presented in textbooks, articles, or lectures. Identify any logical flaws or fallacies and develop counterarguments based on sound reasoning.

7. **Collaborate and Discuss:** Engaging in discussions or study groups with fellow learners can enhance your logical thinking abilities. You refine your reasoning skills and gain new perspectives by exchanging ideas, challenging each other's assumptions, and defending your viewpoints.

By incorporating these strategies into your study routine, you can harness the power of logical thinking to unlock your full potential. Whether you are a businessman/woman seeking to make informed decisions, a student aiming for academic success, or an athlete looking for a competitive edge, logical thinking will undoubtedly enhance your learning experience and overall cognitive abilities. Remember, logical thinking is a skill that can be cultivated through practice and perseverance – embrace it, and the possibilities are endless.

APPLYING LOGICAL THINKING TO PROBLEM-SOLVING IN SCHOOL

In today's fast-paced and complex world, the ability to think logically and solve problems is more crucial than ever. Whether you are a businessman/woman, a mom, a student, a worker, a politician, or an athlete, logical thinking skills are indispensable for success in various aspects of life. This subchapter aims to explore the importance of applying logical thinking to problem-solving, specifically in the context of schools and educational settings.

Logical thinking is a process that involves systematic reasoning, analysis, and evaluation of information to arrive at sound conclusions. It enables individuals to approach problems with clarity, objectivity, and critical thinking. In the realm of education, logical thinking plays a vital role in enhancing academic performance, fostering creativity, and developing problem-solving abilities.

One of the key benefits of applying logical thinking to problem-solving in school is the development of analytical skills. Students can effectively identify the underlying issues and devise practical solutions by learning to break down complex issues into smaller, more manageable parts. This approach allows them to approach academic challenges with a logical framework, helping them to excel in subjects ranging from mathematics to language arts.

Logical thinking empowers students to think independently and critically evaluate the information presented to them. It enables them to question assumptions, identify biases, and draw reliable conclusions based on evidence and logical reasoning. By honing these skills, students become active participants in their education, capable of analyzing and evaluating the information they encounter, thus fostering a deeper understanding and appreciation for the subjects they study.

Studies show, logical thinking promotes creativity and innovation in problem-solving. By encouraging students to explore multiple perspectives, consider alternative solutions, and explore unconventional solutions, they become more adept at finding unique and effective approaches to challenges. This enhances their academic performance and equips them with valuable skills that are highly sought after in the professional world.

Applying logical thinking to problem-solving in school is essential for individuals across various walks of life. Students, businessmen/women, Mothers, workers, public servants, and athletes can unlock their full potential, achieve academic success, enhance their problem-solving abilities, and foster creativity by cultivating logical thinking skills. With logical thinking as their guiding compass, individuals can navigate the complexities of the modern world with confidence and competence.

CHAPTER 7

LOGICAL THINKING IN THE WORKPLACE: USING LOGICAL THINKING FOR EFFICIENT TIME MANAGEMENT

Time management is a crucial skill that everyone, regardless of their profession or background, needs to master. Effectively managing your time can greatly enhance your productivity and success. And when it comes to time management, logical thinking can be a powerful tool to help you unlock your full potential.

Logical thinking is a structured approach that involves analyzing situations and making decisions based on sound reasoning and evidence. By applying logical thinking to time management, you can identify priorities, eliminate unnecessary tasks, and focus on what truly matters. Here are some strategies that can help you harness the power of logical thinking for efficient time management:

1. **Goal Setting:** Start by setting clear and specific goals for yourself. Logical thinking can help you evaluate the importance and feasibility of each goal, allowing you to prioritize them accordingly. Setting realistic goals allows you to allocate your time more effectively and avoid wasting it on irrelevant tasks.

2. **Prioritization:** Once you have defined your goals, use logical thinking to determine which tasks are most critical to achieving them. Evaluate the urgency, importance, and potential impact of each task, and allocate your time accordingly. This approach ensures that you focus on high-priority activities and avoid getting overwhelmed by less important ones.

3. **Time Blocking:** Logical thinking can help you create a structured schedule by breaking your day into manageable blocks of time. Assign specific tasks or activities to each block, allowing for flexibility and accounting for unexpected

events. This method helps you stay organized, reduces procrastination, and ensures that you allocate sufficient time to each task.

4. **Decision-Making:** Logical thinking can assist you in making efficient decisions regarding time allocation. By evaluating the potential outcomes and consequences of each choice, you can prioritize tasks that offer the highest value and align with your goals. This approach helps you avoid time-consuming distractions and focus on tasks that bring you closer to your objectives.

5. **Reflection and Adaptation:** Regularly reflect on your time management strategies and assess their effectiveness. Logical thinking allows you to analyze your achievements, identify areas for improvement, and make necessary adjustments. You can optimize your time management skills and achieve greater efficiency by continuously adapting your approach.

By incorporating logical thinking into your time management practices, you can streamline your workflow, reduce stress, and achieve more in less time. Whether you are a busy professional, a parent juggling multiple responsibilities, a student facing deadlines, or anyone seeking enhanced productivity, logical thinking is a powerful tool that can unlock your full potential. Embrace the power of logical thinking and take control of your time to achieve greater success and fulfillment in all aspects of your life.

PROBLEM-SOLVING AND DECISION-MAKING IN THE WORKPLACE

In the workplace, the ability to effectively solve problems and make sound decisions is crucial for success. Having strong problem-solving and decision-making skills can greatly enhance your performance and help you achieve your goals. This subchapter will delve into the importance of logic and logical thinking in problem-solving and decision-making, providing you with valuable insights and practical techniques to unlock your full potential.

Logic and logical thinking form the foundation of problem-solving processes. By applying logical reasoning, you can identify the root causes of problems, evaluate potential solutions, and make informed decisions. This skill is invaluable in the workplace as it allows you to navigate complex situations, resolve conflicts, and achieve optimal outcomes.

Throughout this subchapter, we will explore various strategies to enhance your logical thinking abilities. We will delve into the principles of deductive and inductive reasoning, teaching you how to analyze information, identify patterns, and draw logical conclusions. By mastering these techniques, you will be able to approach problem-solving with clarity and precision.

We will address the importance of critical thinking in decision-making. We will discuss how biases, emotions, and cognitive traps can cloud judgment and hinder rational decision-making. By understanding these pitfalls, you will be equipped to make more objective decisions and minimize the impact of cognitive biases.

Here we will provide you with practical tools to enhance your problem-solving and decision-making abilities. We will introduce frameworks such as the SWOT analysis, decision matrices, and brainstorming techniques, empowering you to systematically approach problems and evaluate potential solutions.

By honing your logical thinking skills, you will not only become a more effective difficulty solver and decision-maker, but also gain a competitive edge in the workplace. Employers value individuals who can think critically, analyze data, and provide innovative solutions. Whether you are an aspiring entrepreneur, a dedicated professional, or a student preparing for the workforce, this subchapter will equip you with the necessary tools to excel in your chosen field.

Ultimately, the ability to solve problems and make informed decisions is a lifelong skill that extends far beyond the workplace. Logic and logical thinking can benefit all aspects of your life, from personal relationships to financial decisions. By embracing the power of logical thinking, you will unlock your full potential and pave the way for success in all areas of your life.

ENHANCING LEADERSHIP SKILLS WITH LOGICAL THINKING

Leadership skills are crucial for success in any field or profession. The ability to lead effectively is essential. But what sets great leaders apart from the rest? The answer lies in the power of logical thinking.

Logical thinking is the process of using reasoning and critical thinking to make sound decisions and solve problems. It is an invaluable skill that can be honed and applied to various aspects of life. When it comes to leadership, logical thinking can be the key to unlocking your full potential and becoming a more effective leader.

One of the primary benefits of logical thinking for leaders is the ability to make well-informed decisions. Logical thinking allows you to analyze situations objectively, weigh the pros and cons, and consider all relevant factors before reaching a conclusion. This rational approach to decision-making minimizes the influence of emotions or biases and leads to more effective outcomes.

Logical thinking enables leaders to effectively communicate their ideas and strategies. Leaders can convey their thoughts clearly and concisely by using logical reasoning and presenting well-structured arguments. This ensures that their message is understood and inspires confidence and trust among their team members or followers. Additionally, logical thinking helps leaders anticipate potential obstacles or challenges and develop contingency plans. By considering different scenarios and their potential outcomes, leaders can proactively prepare for any eventualities, mitigate risks, and maintain a strategic advantage.

Logical thinking fosters innovation and problem-solving skills. Leaders who can think logically are better equipped to identify patterns, spot opportunities, and devise creative solutions to complex challenges. They can break down complex problems into manageable parts, analyze them systematically, and arrive at effective solutions.

To enhance your leadership skills with logical thinking, it is essential to continuously develop and sharpen your reasoning abilities. This can be achieved through various means, such as reading books on logic, attending logic-based workshops or seminars, and practicing logical thinking exercises.

Logical thinking is a powerful tool that can significantly enhance your leadership skills. By leveraging the principles of logic and critical thinking, leaders can make better decisions, communicate more effectively, anticipate challenges, and solve problems creatively. Regardless of your profession or background, incorporating logical thinking into your leadership approach will undoubtedly unlock your full potential and set you apart as a successful and influential leader.

CHAPTER 8

LOGICAL THINKING FOR PUBLIC SERVANTS: THE ROLE OF LOGICAL THINKING IN POLITICAL DECISION-MAKING

In the realm of politics, decisions hold immense power, as they shape the course of nations and impact the lives of countless individuals. To navigate the complex landscape of governance effectively, political decision-makers must rely on logical thinking. In this subchapter, we explore the profound role of logical thinking in political decision-making and how it empowers individuals across diverse backgrounds and professions.

1. THE FOUNDATION OF LOGICAL THINKING

Logical thinking serves as the foundation for sound decision-making in politics. It involves analyzing arguments, evaluating evidence, and drawing conclusions based on rationality rather than emotions or biases. By adhering to logical principles, political decision-makers can ensure that their choices are based on facts, reason, and objective analysis.

2. ENHANCING CRITICAL ANALYSIS

Logical thinking equips individuals with the ability to critically analyze political issues and policies. Businessmen/women can assess the economic implications of certain decisions, while Mothers and students can evaluate the impact on social welfare and education. Workers can gauge the effects on employment, and athletes can consider the role of politics in sports. By employing logical thinking, individuals from all walks of life can contribute to informed political discussions and decision-making.

3. OVERCOMING COGNITIVE BIASES

Public servants are not immune to cognitive biases, which can cloud judgment and hinder effective decision-making. Logical thinking helps identify and overcome these biases, allowing decision-makers to approach political issues objectively and without undue influence. By utilizing logical reasoning, public servants can make decisions that prioritize the common good over personal or partisan interests.

4. FOSTERING TRANSPARENCY AND ACCOUNTABILITY

Logical thinking promotes transparency and accountability in political decision-making. When Public servants rely on logical reasoning, their actions and justifications become more coherent and transparent to the public. This fosters trust and allows citizens to hold their representatives accountable for their decisions, ensuring a more democratic and responsive political system.

5. PROMOTING COLLABORATION AND COMPROMISE

Political decision-making often requires collaboration and compromise. Logical thinking facilitates constructive dialogue among diverse stakeholders, enabling them to explore common ground and develop mutually beneficial solutions. By transcending personal or ideological differences, political decision-makers can arrive at policies that address the needs and aspirations of a wider population.

In the dynamic world of politics, logical thinking plays a pivotal role in shaping decisions that impact societies at large. From businessmen/women to Mothers, students to workers, and athletes to public servants, the power of logical thinking empowers individuals across all professions and backgrounds to engage in informed political decision-making. By embracing logical thinking, we can unlock our full potential as active participants in shaping a better future for our communities and nations.

ANALYZING AND EVALUATING POLICIES WITH LOGICAL THINKING

Policies play a crucial role in shaping our societies and organizations. Whether you are a businessman/woman, a mom, a student, a worker, a politician, or an athlete, understanding how to analyze and evaluate policies through logical thinking is essential for making informed decisions and maximizing your potential.

Logical thinking is a powerful tool that enables us to examine policies critically, identify flaws, and propose effective solutions. It allows us to dissect policies systematically, focusing on their underlying assumptions, evidence, and potential consequences. By employing logical thinking, we can avoid falling into the trap of accepting policies without questioning their rationale and impact.

The first step in analyzing policies is to break them down into their basic components. This involves identifying the policy's objectives, the methods used to achieve those objectives, and the stakeholders involved. By dissecting policies in this way, we can gain a comprehensive understanding of their purpose and scope.

Once we have a clear grasp of the policy's components, we can employ logical thinking to evaluate its effectiveness. This includes examining the evidence and data supporting the policy, assessing its potential consequences, and considering alternative approaches that could achieve the desired outcomes. Logical thinking allows us to weigh the pros and cons objectively, ensuring that our evaluations are based on sound reasoning rather than personal biases.

Logical thinking also enables us to identify any logical fallacies or inconsistencies within policies. We can pinpoint areas that require further scrutiny or modification by recognizing faulty reasoning, such as hasty generalizations or false cause and effect relationships. This critical evaluation helps us refine policies, making them more robust and efficient.

Logical thinking empowers us to propose innovative and evidence-based alternatives to existing policies. By leveraging our analytical skills, we can identify creative solutions that address the root causes of problems while considering the potential risks and benefits. This ability to embrace innovative approaches is invaluable in an ever-changing world where new challenges constantly arise.

Analyzing and evaluating policies with logical thinking is a fundamental skill that unlocks our full potential. It allows us to make informed decisions, challenge the existing state of affairs, and suggest effective solutions. By employing logical thinking, businessmen/women, Mothers, students, workers, public servants, and athletes can navigate the complexities of policymaking, enhancing their ability to succeed in their respective fields. Logic and logical thinking are not only niches but essential tools for success in today's dynamic world.

PUBLIC SPEAKING AND PERSUASION TECHNIQUES WITH LOGICAL THINKING

Effective communication and persuasive skills are crucial for success in various domains. The ability to speak with confidence and convince others through logical thinking is essential. This subchapter aims to equip individuals in the niches of logic and logical thinking with powerful public speaking and persuasion techniques.

1. THE ART OF PUBLIC SPEAKING

Public speaking is an art that can be mastered with practice and the right techniques. It involves delivering speeches, presentations, or pitches to an audience. This section will delve into the significance of public speaking and provide valuable tips on how to improve your performance, such as voice modulation, body language, and engaging storytelling.

2. UNDERSTANDING PERSUASION

Persuasion is a skill that allows you to influence others' thoughts, actions, and decisions. By incorporating logical thinking into your persuasive techniques, you can enhance your effectiveness exponentially. This section will explore various aspects of persuasion, including the psychology behind it and the use of logical arguments to convince others.

3.   LOGICAL THINKING IN PUBLIC SPEAKING

Logical thinking is the foundation of effective communication. By employing logical reasoning and critical thinking skills, you can present your ideas in a clear, concise, and convincing manner. This section will provide practical strategies for incorporating logical thinking into your public speaking, such as structuring your speech logically, using evidence-based arguments, and anticipating counterarguments.

4.   THE POWER OF RHETORIC

Rhetoric is the art of using language effectively to persuade and captivate an audience. By combining logical thinking with rhetorical techniques, you can make your speeches more compelling and influential. This section will explore key rhetorical devices, such as ethos, logos, and pathos, and how to utilize them to enhance your persuasive abilities.

5. OVERCOMING STAGE FRIGHT

Stage fright is a common fear that can hinder effective public speaking. This section will offer valuable advice on overcoming stage fright, such as visualization techniques, deep breathing exercises, and the power of positive self-talk. By mastering these techniques, you can confidently deliver powerful speeches that leave a lasting impact.

In business, family life, academia, politics, and sports, the ability to speak persuasively and employ logical thinking is indispensable. This subchapter has provided valuable insights and techniques to help individuals in the niches of logic and logical thinking enhance their public speaking skills and persuasion abilities. By applying these strategies, you can unlock your full potential and achieve success in all areas of life.

LOGICAL THINKING FOR ATHLETES: ENHANCING PERFORMANCE THROUGH LOGICAL THINKING

S uccess in any field requires not only hard work and determination, but also the ability to think critically and make sound decisions. Logical thinking is a powerful tool that can help individuals from all walks of life achieve their goals and unlock their full potential. This subchapter explores the ways in which logical thinking can enhance performance in various domains, catering to the diverse audience of businessmen/women, Mothers, students, workers, public servants, and athletes.

For businessmen/women, logical thinking can provide a competitive edge by improving problem-solving skills, enabling effective decision-making, and fostering innovation. By approaching challenges with a logical mindset, business professionals can analyze various options, assess risks, and identify the most favorable outcomes.

Logical thinking helps in identifying patterns and trends in market data, enabling entrepreneurs to make informed and strategic business moves. Mothers, as primary caregivers, juggle numerous responsibilities daily. Logical thinking can assist them in managing their tasks efficiently, prioritizing activities, and finding creative solutions to common parenting issues. By applying logical reasoning, Mothers can establish routines, set realistic goals, and make informed parenting choices. It also helps in fostering critical thinking skills in their children, equipping them with essential problem-solving abilities from an early age.

For students, logical thinking is an essential skill for academic success. It aids in understanding complex concepts, analyzing information, and formulating coherent arguments. By approaching their studies with a logical mindset, students can grasp difficult subjects more easily, excel in exams, and develop a lifelong love for learning.

Workers in any field can benefit from logical thinking. It enhances their ability to analyze work processes, identify inefficiencies, and propose effective solutions. By thinking logically, workers can streamline their tasks, increase productivity, and contribute to the overall success of their organization.

Public servants, too, can leverage logical thinking to make informed policy decisions, evaluate the consequences of their actions, and communicate their ideas effectively to the public. By employing logical reasoning, public servants can build strong arguments, debate effectively, and make decisions that benefit their constituents.

Even athletes can harness the power of logical thinking to enhance their performance. By analyzing their opponents' strengths and weaknesses, developing effective strategies, and making split-second decisions on the field, athletes can gain a competitive edge and achieve their athletic goals.

Logical thinking is a versatile and powerful tool that can benefit individuals from all walks of life. By enhancing problem-solving abilities, decision-making skills, and critical thinking, logical thinking empowers businessmen/women, Mothers, students, workers, public servants, and athletes to unlock their full potential and achieve success in their respective domains.

DEVELOPING MENTAL RESILIENCE WITH LOGICAL THINKING

Mental resilience has become a vital skill for individuals from all walks of life. Whether you are a businessman/woman, a mom, a student, a worker, a politician, or an athlete, the ability to overcome challenges and bounce back from setbacks is crucial for success and well-being. Logical thinking is a powerful tool that can help you develop and strengthen your mental resilience.

Logical thinking is the process of using reason and rationality to analyze situations, solve problems, and make informed decisions. It involves breaking down complex issues into smaller, manageable parts and systematically evaluating each component. By applying logical thinking to your daily life, you can cultivate a resilient mindset that enables you to navigate through obstacles more effectively.

One of the key benefits of logical thinking is its ability to help you maintain a balanced perspective during challenging times. When faced with adversity, it is easy to become overwhelmed by emotions and lose sight of the bigger picture. Logical thinking allows you to detach yourself from the immediate emotional response and assess the situation objectively. By examining the facts and evidence, you can gain clarity and make more rational choices, ultimately enhancing your ability to bounce back from setbacks.

Logical thinking equips you with problem-solving skills that are essential for building mental resilience. It encourages you to approach problems systematically, breaking them down into smaller, more manageable components. By identifying the root causes and analyzing potential solutions, you can develop a strategic plan of action. This logical problem-solving approach allows you to tackle challenges with a sense of purpose and confidence, enabling you to persevere in the face of adversity.

In addition to enhancing your problem-solving abilities, logical thinking also promotes adaptability and flexibility. You become more open to alternative perspectives and new ideas by embracing a logical mindset. This ability to think critically and consider different viewpoints allows you to adapt your strategies and approaches when faced with unexpected obstacles. It enables you to adjust your thinking and find creative solutions, ultimately strengthening your mental resilience.

Whether you are a businessman/woman striving for success, a mom juggling multiple responsibilities, a student facing academic pressures, or striving for career advancement, an athlete pushing your physical limits. The need to develop mental resilience through logical thinking is a valuable skill. By cultivating a logical mindset, you can approach challenges with confidence, maintain a balanced perspective, and adapt to changing circumstances. So, embrace the power of logical thinking and unlock your full potential to thrive in today's dynamic world.

SETTING AND ACHIEVING GOALS WITH LOGICAL THINKING

Setting goals and achieving them has become more crucial than ever before. Whether you are a businessperson, a mom, a student, a worker, a politician, or an athlete, having the ability to set and achieve goals can significantly impact your success and overall well-being. This subchapter, titled "Setting and Achieving Goals with Logical Thinking," delves into the power of logical thinking in the process of goal setting and provides valuable insights to individuals within the niches of logic and logical thinking.

Logical thinking involves the use of reason and rationality to analyze situations and make informed decisions. By applying logical thinking to goal setting, individuals can enhance their ability to envision, plan, and execute their objectives effectively. This subchapter explores how logical thinking can serve as a powerful tool for setting realistic and achievable goals.

The content begins by highlighting the importance of clarity and specificity when setting goals. Logical thinking emphasizes the need for clear, well-defined objectives that can be broken down into smaller, manageable tasks. It provides practical techniques for identifying and prioritizing goals, ensuring they align with personal or professional aspirations.

This subchapter delves into the role of logical thinking in assessing the feasibility of goals. By employing logical reasoning, individuals can realistically evaluate their resources, capabilities, and potential obstacles. This aids in setting realistic expectations and developing strategies to overcome challenges efficiently.

The content explores the significance of logical thinking in creating action plans. Logical thinking enables individuals to map out a step-by-step process to achieve their goals. It emphasizes the importance of setting measurable milestones, tracking progress, and making necessary adjustments along the way.

Here, we address the role of logical thinking in maintaining motivation and resilience throughout the goal-setting journey. By employing logical reasoning, individuals can identify potential setbacks and develop contingency plans to stay on track. It provides insights into fostering a growth mindset, embracing failures as learning opportunities, and celebrating successes.

"Setting and Achieving Goals with Logical Thinking" is a subchapter designed to empower businessmen/women, Mothers, students, workers, public servants, and athletes who are interested in enhancing their logical thinking skills. By applying logical thinking to goal setting, individuals can unlock their full potential and achieve both personal and professional success. This subchapter serves as a comprehensive guide, equipping readers with practical strategies to set clear, realistic goals, assess feasibility, create actionable plans, and maintain motivation and resilience throughout their journey.

CHAPTER 10

OVERCOMING LOGICAL FALLACIES: RECOGNIZING AND AVOIDING COMMON LOGICAL FALLACIES

Information is constantly bombarding us from all directions; it has become more crucial than ever to develop our logical thinking skills. Whether you are a businessman/woman, a mom, a student, a worker, a politician, or an athlete, the ability to recognize and avoid common logical fallacies is essential in making sound decisions, solving problems, and effectively communicating your ideas.

Logical fallacies are errors in reasoning that can lead to flawed conclusions or deceptive arguments. They often rely on emotions, biases, or faulty logic to manipulate our thinking process. By being aware of these fallacies, we can protect ourselves from being swayed by misleading information and faulty arguments.

One common fallacy is the ad hominem, which occurs when someone attacks an individual's character or personal traits instead of addressing their argument. In the business world, this fallacy can manifest as personal attacks on competitors rather than focusing on the strengths of one's own product or service. By recognizing this fallacy, businessmen/women can engage in more productive and respectful discussions that foster healthy competition.

Another prevalent fallacy is the appeal to authority, where someone claims that a statement is true simply because an authority figure said so. This can be seen in politics, where public servants may use the endorsement of a popular figure to justify their policies without providing substantial evidence. By critically evaluating the evidence behind claims, public servants can establish credibility and gain the trust of their constituents.

For students, understanding the slippery slope fallacy is vital. This fallacy occurs when someone argues that a particular action will inevitably lead to a series of negative consequences. Students can develop a more nuanced understanding of cause and effect by identifying this fallacy, allowing them to make informed decisions based on evidence rather than fear mongering.

Lastly, athletes can benefit greatly from recognizing the fallacy of false cause, which assumes a cause-and-effect relationship between two events without sufficient evidence. By avoiding this fallacy, athletes can make informed training decisions and avoid wasting time and energy on ineffective practices.

By being aware of these common logical fallacies and training our minds to think critically, we can unlock our full potential in all aspects of life. Whether we are in business, parenting, education, politics, or sports, logical thinking enables us to make informed decisions, solve complex problems, and communicate effectively. So, let us embrace the power of logical thinking and equip ourselves with the tools to recognize and avoid these common logical fallacies.

STRATEGIES FOR DEBUNKING FALSE ARGUMENTS

It is essential to possess the skills required to detect and debunk false arguments. Whether you are a businessman/woman, a mom, a student, a worker, a politician, or an athlete, logical thinking is a valuable tool that can help you navigate through the sea of misinformation and make informed decisions. This subchapter aims to equip you with effective strategies to identify and dismantle false arguments, enabling you to unlock your full potential in the realm of logic and logical thinking.

1. **Recognize logical fallacies:** Logical fallacies are common errors in reasoning that can lead to false arguments. You can pinpoint their presence in discussions or debates by familiarizing yourself with these fallacies – such as ad hominem attacks, straw man arguments, and false cause fallacies. Understanding fallacies

allows you to expose flawed reasoning and strengthen your arguments.

2. **Ask critical questions:** When confronted with an argument, ask yourself critical questions to evaluate its validity. Is there evidence to support the claim? Are there any logical inconsistencies? Does the argument rely on emotions rather than facts? By adopting a skeptical mindset and probing deeper, you can effectively uncover weak points and challenge false arguments.

3. **Research and fact-check:** In the age of information, it is crucial to verify the credibility of sources and the accuracy of claims. Take the time to conduct thorough research and fact-check the information presented. Seek reputable sources, cross-reference multiple perspectives, and critically analyze the evidence provided. By doing so, you can expose false arguments and arm yourself with accurate information.

4. **Present counter arguments:** One of the most effective ways to debunk false arguments is by presenting counter arguments. By offering alternative perspectives backed by logical

reasoning and evidence, you can challenge the validity of the initial argument. Presenting well-thought-out counterarguments encourages a healthy exchange of ideas and helps others see the flaws in false arguments.

5. **Cultivate rational thinking:** To become a master of logical thinking, it is essential to cultivate rational thinking as a habit. This involves being aware of your biases, avoiding emotional reasoning, and focusing on evidence-based conclusions. You can navigate complex discussions and distinguish between valid arguments and false claims by honing your rational thinking skills.

The ability to debunk false arguments is a valuable skill that cuts across various domains of life. By employing strategies such as recognizing logical fallacies, asking critical questions, conducting thorough research, presenting counterarguments, and cultivating rational thinking, you can become a logical thinking powerhouse. Empowered with these strategies, businessmen/women, Mothers, students, workers, public servants, and athletes alike can unlock their full potential and make informed decisions in an increasingly complex world.

PROMOTING RATIONAL DISCUSSIONS AND DEBATES

Today, emotional reactions often dominate our conversations, the art of rational discussions and debates is more important than ever. Whether you are a businessman/woman, a mom, a student, a worker, a politician, or an athlete, the ability to engage in logical thinking and communicate effectively is essential for personal and professional growth. This subchapter, titled "Promoting Rational Discussions and Debates," will equip you with the necessary tools to navigate through complex discussions and foster constructive debates.

First and foremost, it is crucial to establish a foundation of respect and open-mindedness. Rational discussions can only flourish when all parties involved are willing to listen to different perspectives and consider alternative viewpoints. We create an environment that encourages critical thinking and innovation by valuing diverse opinions. This mindset is especially valuable in business settings, where diverse teams can generate groundbreaking ideas and solutions.

To promote rational discussions, it is essential to develop strong reasoning and logical thinking skills. This involves the ability to analyze information objectively, identify biases, and question assumptions. We can separate fact from opinion, evaluate evidence, and draw well-informed conclusions by employing logical reasoning. These skills are not limited to any specific field or profession; they are applicable to all aspects of life.

Effective communication plays a pivotal role in promoting rational discussions. You can express your thoughts clearly and concisely by honing your communication skills while actively listening to others. Active listening involves paying attention, asking thoughtful questions, and seeking clarification when necessary. By fostering an atmosphere of open dialogue, we create opportunities for growth, learning, and collaboration.

It is important to remember that rational discussions and debates are not about winning or proving someone wrong. Instead, they should focus on exploring different perspectives and finding common ground. By emphasizing the goal of reaching a shared understanding, we can build bridges between individuals with varying viewpoints, leading to better decision-making and problem-solving.

"Promoting Rational Discussions and Debates" aims to equip individuals from various backgrounds, including businessmen/women, Mothers, students, workers, public servants, and athletes, with the necessary tools to engage in logical thinking and effective communication. By valuing diverse opinions, developing reasoning skills, and fostering open dialogue, we can unlock our full potential and contribute to a more rational, informed, and collaborative society.

THE POWER OF LOGICAL THINKING IN EVERYDAY LIFE: APPLYING LOGICAL THINKING TO PERSONAL RELATIONSHIPS

Personal relationships have become more complex than ever before. Whether you are a businessman/woman, a mom, a student, a worker, a politician, or an athlete, the ability to navigate and nurture relationships is crucial for success and overall well-being. This subchapter aims to introduce you to the power of logical thinking in enhancing your personal relationships.

Logic and logical thinking are not limited to solving math problems or philosophical debates.

They can be applied to better understand, communicate, and resolve conflicts in our relationships. By approaching our interactions with a logical mindset, we can avoid misunderstandings, manage emotions effectively, and foster healthier connections with others. One of the fundamental principles of logical thinking is clarity. It is important to clearly define what we expect from our relationships and what we are willing to contribute. By setting clear boundaries and expectations, we can avoid unnecessary conflicts and ensure both parties are on the same page.

Another aspect of logical thinking in personal relationships is objective analysis. Instead of jumping to conclusions or making assumptions, we should strive to gather all the relevant information and evaluate situations objectively. By doing so, we can make more informed decisions and avoid impulsive reactions that may harm our relationships.

Logical thinking also encourages effective communication. It emphasizes the importance of active listening, empathy, and open-mindedness. We can avoid misunderstandings and build stronger connections by actively listening to others and considering their perspective. Additionally, logical thinking prompts us to express our thoughts and emotions in a clear and assertive manner, promoting healthy dialogue and problem-solving.

Conflict resolution is another area where logical thinking can be highly beneficial. Instead of resorting to heated arguments or silent treatments, logical thinking encourages us to approach conflicts with a problem-solving mindset. By identifying the core issues, analyzing the potential solutions, and considering the long-term consequences, we can find compromises that satisfy both parties and strengthen the relationship.

Applying logical thinking to personal relationships can significantly enhance our ability to navigate the complexities of human connections. Whether you are a businessman/woman, a mom, a student, a worker, a politician, or an athlete, the power of logical thinking can empower you to communicate effectively, resolve conflicts, and foster healthier relationships. By embracing logical thinking, you can unlock your full potential in both your personal and professional life.

RESOLVING CONFLICTS WITH LOGICAL THINKING

Conflicts are an inevitable part of life, and they often arise in various aspects of our lives, be it at work, home, school, or even within ourselves. However, conflicts don't have to lead to negative outcomes or damaged relationships. By employing logical thinking, we can effectively resolve conflicts and turn them into opportunities for growth and understanding.

In "Resolving Conflicts", we will explore the power of logical thinking in resolving conflicts and provide practical strategies that can be applied by businessmen/women, Mothers, students, workers, public servants, athletes, and anyone interested in enhancing their logical thinking skills.

Logical thinking enables us to separate emotions from facts, allowing us to approach conflicts with rationality and objectivity. By analyzing the situation from multiple perspectives, we can gain a comprehensive understanding of the conflict and identify the underlying causes. This understanding forms the foundation for finding mutually beneficial solutions.

One crucial aspect of resolving conflicts with logical thinking is effective communication. We will delve into the importance of active listening, empathy, and clear expression of thoughts and feelings. These skills foster better understanding and promote a harmonious and constructive environment for conflict resolution.

We will discuss various conflict resolution techniques that are rooted in logical thinking. These techniques include mediation, negotiation, compromise, and problem-solving. By applying these methods, individuals can achieve win-win outcomes where both parties feel satisfied with the resolution.

Additionally, this subchapter will address the role of emotions in conflicts and how logical thinking can help manage and control emotional responses. By recognizing and understanding our emotions, we can prevent them from clouding our judgment and hindering the resolution process.

We will explore case studies and real-life examples where logical thinking played a pivotal role in resolving conflicts successfully. These stories will inspire and motivate readers to embrace logical thinking as a powerful tool in their personal and professional lives.

By harnessing the power of logical thinking, you can unlock your full potential and transform conflicts into opportunities for growth, understanding, and stronger relationships.

ENHANCING PROBLEM-SOLVING SKILLS IN DAILY LIFE

Problem-solving skills have become more crucial than ever. Whether you are a businessman/woman, a mom, a student, a worker, a politician, or an athlete, the ability to think logically and solve problems efficiently is essential for success in any field. This subchapter aims to provide you with valuable insights and tips on how to enhance your problem-solving skills, empowering you to overcome challenges and unlock your full potential.

Logic and logical thinking form the foundation of problem-solving. By understanding the principles of logical reasoning, you can approach problems with a structured and systematic approach. The Power of Logical Thinking will guide you through the process, helping you develop your analytical skills and make better decisions in your personal and professional life.

One key aspect of logical thinking is recognizing patterns and connections. By training your mind to spot these patterns, you will be able to identify underlying issues and find effective solutions. The book will introduce you to various techniques, such as brainstorming, mind mapping, and critical thinking exercises, to sharpen your ability to see connections and explore unconventional solutions.

Another essential skill for problem-solving is breaking down complex problems into smaller, manageable parts. This approach allows you to tackle each component individually, leading to a more systematic and organized problem-solving process. The book will provide you with practical examples and strategies to help you break down problems effectively, enabling you to approach them with confidence and clarity.

So, effective problem-solving requires a logical evaluation of available options and potential outcomes. The Power of Logical Thinking will teach you how to objectively assess the pros and cons of alternative solutions, enabling you to make informed decisions. By understanding the logical consequences of your choices, you can navigate through challenges and optimize your results.

Solving skills will highlight the importance of practice and continuous improvement in problem-solving. By incorporating logical thinking exercises and real-life case studies, the book will provide you with ample opportunities to apply your problem-solving skills and refine them further. Remember, problem-solving is a skill that can be honed and mastered with dedication and perseverance.

Whether you are a businessman/woman seeking innovative solutions, a mom managing daily challenges, a student striving for academic excellence, a worker facing professional obstacles, a politician tackling complex issues, or an athlete aiming for peak performance. The Power of Logical Thinking will equip you with the tools to enhance your problem-solving skills and unlock your full potential. Embrace logical thinking, and let it guide you towards success in every aspect of your life.

CHAPTER 12

HARNESSING YOUR FULL LOGICAL THINKING POTENTIAL: CONTINUOUS IMPROVEMENT AND PRACTICE FOR LOGICAL THINKING

The ability to think logically is a crucial skill that can significantly impact our personal and professional lives. Whether you are a businessman/woman, a mom, a student, a worker, a politician, or an athlete, logical thinking is applicable and beneficial to all aspects of life. This subchapter explores the importance of continuous improvement and practice for enhancing logical thinking abilities.

Logical thinking is the process of reasoning, analyzing, and evaluating information in a systematic and rational manner. It enables individuals to make sound decisions, solve complex problems, and communicate effectively. However, logical thinking is not an innate trait; it is a skill that can be developed and honed through continuous improvement and practice.

Individuals need to adopt a growth mindset to cultivate and strengthen logical thinking abilities.

Embracing the belief that intelligence and skills can be developed fosters a willingness to learn and persevere. Dedicate time to expand your knowledge in various domains, expose yourself to new ideas, and engage in critical thinking exercises. Challenge yourself to solve puzzles, riddles, or brainteasers regularly. This practice helps to exercise your mind, sharpen your analytical skills, and improve your ability to think logically.

Seek opportunities to engage in logical reasoning activities. Join debating clubs, attend seminars or workshops on critical thinking, and participate in group discussions. Engaging in these activities allows you to explore different perspectives, analyze arguments, and enhance your logical thinking skills. Furthermore, consider taking courses or enrolling in online programs that specifically focus on logical thinking. These educational resources provide structured guidance and practical exercises to help you develop a solid foundation in logical thinking.

It is essential to continuously evaluate and reflect on your decision-making processes. Analyze the outcomes of your decisions and identify areas for improvement. Take note of any biases, fallacies, or cognitive errors that may have influenced your thinking. By acknowledging and rectifying these shortcomings, you can refine your logical thinking skills and make better-informed choices in the future.

Logical thinking is a vital skill that can benefit individuals from all walks of life. You can enhance your logical thinking abilities by embracing a growth mindset and committing to continuous improvement and practice. Engage in various activities that challenge your mind, seek opportunities to engage in logical reasoning, and reflect on your decision-making processes. Developing strong logical thinking skills will empower you to navigate through life's complexities, make informed decisions, and unlock your full potential.

OVERCOMING CHALLENGES AND OBSTACLES IN DEVELOPING LOGICAL THINKING SKILLS

The ability to think logically has become an essential skill for success in various aspects of life. Whether you are a businessman/woman, a mom, a student, a worker, a politician, or an athlete, logical thinking can significantly enhance your decision-making, problem-solving, and critical analysis abilities. However, developing these skills is not always an easy task. In this subchapter, we will explore the challenges and obstacles that individuals may encounter on their journey to developing logical thinking skills and provide practical strategies to overcome them.

One of the most common challenges in developing logical thinking skills is the presence of cognitive biases. These biases are ingrained patterns of thinking that can cloud our judgment and lead us to make irrational decisions. To overcome this challenge, it is crucial to first recognize and understand these biases. By becoming aware of our own cognitive biases, we can consciously challenge and question our thoughts, ensuring a more logical and rational approach to problem-solving.

Another obstacle to developing logical thinking skills is the lack of practice and exposure to logical reasoning. Many individuals are not accustomed to thinking critically and analytically, as our education systems often prioritize rote memorization over logical thinking. To overcome this obstacle, it is essential to engage in activities that promote logical thinking, such as puzzles, brainteasers, and logic games. Additionally, seeking opportunities to engage in debates or discussions can enhance your logical thinking skills by exposing you to different perspectives and challenging your beliefs.

Time constraints and a busy lifestyle can also pose challenges in the development of logical thinking skills. However, it is important to carve out dedicated time for practicing and honing these skills. Setting aside even a few minutes each day to solve a logic puzzle or analyze a problem can make a significant difference in your ability to think logically over time.

Lastly, fear of failure and the discomfort of uncertainty can hinder the development of logical thinking skills. It is essential to embrace these challenges as opportunities for growth and learning. Recognize that making mistakes and facing uncertainty are natural parts of the learning process. By reframing these challenges as steppingstones to success, you can cultivate a growth mindset that encourages continuous improvement and the development of logical thinking skills.

Developing logical thinking skills is a valuable asset for individuals in various domains of life. By acknowledging and overcoming the challenges and obstacles that may arise, businessmen/women, Mothers, students, workers, public servants, and athletes can unlock their full potential and become more effective decision-makers and problem solvers. With dedication, practice, and a willingness to embrace challenges, anyone can develop and enhance their logical thinking skills, leading to greater success in their personal and professional lives.

INTEGRATING LOGICAL THINKING INTO YOUR PERSONAL AND PROFESSIONAL LIFE

Logical thinking has become an indispensable skill for success in every aspect of life. Whether you are a businessman/woman, a mom, a student, a worker, a politician, or an athlete, the power of logical thinking can unlock your full potential and help you navigate through challenges with ease. This subchapter explores the significance of integrating logical thinking into your personal and professional life, providing practical insights and strategies for harnessing the power of logic.

In the professional realm, logical thinking can be a game-changer. From making strategic decisions to problem-solving, logical thinking allows you to analyze situations objectively, identify patterns, and make sound judgments. By incorporating logical thinking into your approach, you can enhance your problem-solving abilities, streamline your decision-making processes, and ultimately achieve better outcomes. This is particularly crucial for businessmen/women, workers, and public servants who often face complex and high-stakes situations that require critical thinking.

Logical thinking is not limited to professional settings alone; it is equally relevant to personal life. As a mom or a student, logical thinking can help you prioritize tasks, manage your time efficiently, and make informed choices. By analyzing situations logically, you can tackle everyday challenges effectively, balance responsibilities, and achieve personal goals. Logical thinking equips you with the ability to evaluate information critically, enabling you to make informed decisions about health, education, and personal relationships.

Athletes, too, can benefit immensely from integrating logical thinking into their training and performance. By employing logical thinking strategies, athletes can enhance their problem-solving abilities on the field, analyze opponents' strategies, and make split-second decisions. Logical thinking can also help athletes set realistic goals, develop effective training plans, and evaluate their progress objectively.

In integrating, we will delve into various techniques and practices that can help you integrate logical thinking into your personal and professional life. From logical reasoning exercises to decision-making frameworks, you will discover practical tools that can enhance your logical thinking abilities. We will explore real-life examples and case studies to illustrate how logical thinking has transformed the lives and careers of individuals from diverse backgrounds.

By incorporating logical thinking into your life, you can unlock your full potential, overcome challenges, and make informed choices. Whether you are a businessman/woman, a mom, a student, a worker, a politician, or an athlete, the power of logical thinking can revolutionize the way you approach problems and achieve success. Get ready to unleash the power of logical thinking and embark on a journey of personal and professional growth like never before.

CHAPTER 13

RECAP OF THE POWER OF LOGICAL THINKING

We will delve into a recap of the incredible power of logical thinking and how it can help individuals from various walks of life: businessmen/women, Mothers, students, workers, public servants, and athletes: in their respective niches.

Logical thinking forms the foundation of rational decision-making, problem-solving, and critical analysis. It enables individuals to make sense of complex situations, identify patterns, and draw conclusions based on facts and evidence rather than emotions or biases. By embracing logical thinking, individuals can unlock their full potential and achieve remarkable success in their chosen fields.

For businessmen/women, logical thinking is crucial for making sound strategic decisions. It helps them assess risks, evaluate market trends, and identify opportunities for growth. By employing logical thinking, business professionals can develop innovative solutions, streamline processes, and enhance overall efficiency, ultimately leading to increased profitability and success.

Mothers, too, can benefit greatly from logical thinking. Juggling multiple responsibilities, mothers often face countless decisions, big and small, daily. Logical thinking equips them with the ability to prioritize tasks, evaluate options, and make informed choices that benefit both themselves and their families. By employing logical thinking, Mothers can navigate through challenging situations, manage time effectively, and create harmonious environments for their loved ones.

Students can leverage the power of logical thinking to excel academically. It helps them analyze complex problems, understand different subjects, and develop strong analytical skills. Logical thinking enables students to approach exams and assignments with a systematic mindset, thereby enhancing their overall performance and achieving academic success.

Workers across industries can enhance their productivity and efficiency through logical thinking. By organizing tasks logically, workers can improve time management, better allocate resources, and solve problems efficiently. Logical thinking also fosters effective communication and collaboration, enabling workers to contribute meaningfully to their teams and achieve their professional goals.

Logical thinking is equally vital for public servants and athletes. Public servants can use logical thinking to formulate effective policies, analyze complex issues, and communicate their ideas persuasively. On the other hand, athletes can employ logical thinking to strategize their game-plans, analyze opponents' strengths and weaknesses, and improve their overall performance.

Logical thinking is a powerful tool that can benefit individuals from all walks of life, irrespective of their niche. By embracing logical thinking, businessmen/women, Mothers, students, workers, public servants, and athletes can unlock their full potential, make informed decisions, and achieve remarkable success in their respective fields.

RECAP OF KEY CONCEPTS AND SKILLS

We review the fundamental concepts and skills of logical thinking and reasoning in everyday life. Understanding these key principles will equip you with the necessary tools to navigate the complexities of the world around you and make sound decisions.

First and foremost, logical thinking involves the ability to reason and analyze information objectively. It requires you to approach situations with an open mind, free from biases and preconceived notions. By doing so, you can evaluate evidence and draw accurate conclusions based on facts rather than emotions or personal beliefs.

One critical skill of logical thinking is the ability to identify and evaluate arguments. Arguments are the building blocks of logical reasoning. They consist of a series of statements, where one or more premises support a conclusion. Being able to recognize different types of arguments, such as deductive and inductive reasoning, will enable you to assess their validity and strength.

Another essential concept to grasp is the difference between correlation and causation. Often, people mistakenly assume that just because two events occur together, one must be causing the other. However, correlation does not imply causation. Understanding this distinction will help you avoid making faulty assumptions and drawing inaccurate conclusions.

Additionally, critical thinking is closely intertwined with logical thinking. It involves the ability to analyze and evaluate information objectively, considering different perspectives and challenging assumptions. You can enhance your logical reasoning abilities and make well-informed decisions by honing your critical thinking skills.

Logical thinking also incorporates the skill of problem-solving. When faced with a complex issue, the ability to break it down into smaller, manageable parts and systematically analyze each component is crucial. By approaching problems in a logical and systematic manner, you can develop effective solutions and overcome challenges more efficiently.

It is important to understand that logical thinking is not solely an individual endeavor. It has a significant impact on society as a whole. By promoting logical thinking in our communities, we can foster better decision-making, critical analysis, and problem-solving skills among individuals. This collective improvement in logical thinking can lead to a more informed and rational society.

To conclude, this subchapter has provided a recap of the key concepts and skills necessary for logical thinking and reasoning in everyday life. By mastering these principles, you will be better equipped to navigate the complexities of the world, make informed decisions, and contribute to a more logical and rational society.

ENCOURAGEMENT TO APPLY LOGICAL THINKING TO EVERYDAY LIFE

Logic is an essential tool that enables us to navigate the complexities of everyday life. It is not limited to academia or specialized professions; rather, it is a skill that can benefit every individual in society. In this subchapter, we will explore the importance of logical thinking and reasoning in our daily lives and highlight the numerous ways in which it can positively impact our decision-making, problem-solving, and overall well-being.

Logical thinking involves the ability to reason soundly, analyze information critically, and draw valid conclusions. By applying logical thinking in our everyday lives, we can make more informed choices and avoid falling into common traps of faulty reasoning. Whether it is assessing the credibility of news sources, evaluating arguments in a debate, or making financial decisions, logical thinking equips us with the tools to make rational judgments.

One area where logical thinking shines is problem-solving. We can identify the core issues and find effective solutions by breaking down complex problems into smaller, more manageable parts. Logical thinking helps us avoid hasty decisions based on emotions or biases, enabling us to approach issues with a clear and rational mindset.

Furthermore, logical thinking fosters better communication and understanding. We can engage in constructive debates and contribute to meaningful discussions by analyzing and evaluating arguments. It allows us to challenge our assumptions and consider alternative perspectives, leading to more open-mindedness and empathy.

Logical thinking also plays a significant role in our personal growth and well-being. By examining our thoughts and beliefs, we can detect cognitive biases and overcome them. This self-reflection helps us make better choices aligned with our values and goals, leading to a more fulfilling and purposeful life.

In the digital age, where misinformation is widespread, logical thinking is vital. It equips us with the necessary tools to critically evaluate information, separate fact from fiction, and make informed decisions. By cultivating logical thinking skills, we can become responsible consumers of information, contributing to a more informed and educated society. The application of logical thinking in everyday life is crucial for individuals and society as a whole. It empowers us to navigate the complexities of the modern world, make rational decisions, solve problems effectively, and communicate more constructively. By encouraging logical thinking, we can foster a society that values reason, critical analysis, and thoughtful decision-making, leading to a better future for all.

THOUGHTS ON THE IMPORTANCE OF LOGICAL REASONING FOR SOCIETY

Logical reasoning is an essential tool for navigating the complexities of everyday life. It allows individuals to make sound judgments, solve problems, and critically analyze information. In today's fast-paced and information-driven society, the need for logical thinking has become even more crucial. This subchapter aims to underscore the significance of logical reasoning for society and shed light on how it can positively impact our lives.

First and foremost, logical reasoning promotes rational decision-making. By employing logical thinking, individuals can evaluate evidence, weigh pros and cons, and arrive at well-informed choices. In a society where decisions are constantly being made, whether in personal or professional settings, logical reasoning ensures that these decisions are based on sound logic rather than impulsive emotions or biased opinions. This, in turn, leads to more efficient and effective outcomes, benefiting both individuals and society as a whole.

Logical reasoning fosters critical thinking skills. In a world where misinformation and fake news run rampant, the ability to critically analyze information and distinguish between fact and fiction is paramount. Logical reasoning equips individuals with the necessary tools to assess the validity and reliability of information, enabling them to make informed judgments and avoid falling prey to manipulation or deception. This empowers society to be more discerning, knowledgeable, and resistant to misinformation, ultimately fostering a more informed and democratic society.

Logical reasoning encourages problem-solving abilities. Everyday life presents us with a myriad of challenges, both big and small. Logical thinking enables individuals to break down complex problems into smaller, manageable components, allowing for systematic analysis and problem-solving. By approaching problems with a logical mindset, society can find innovative solutions and overcome obstacles more effectively, leading to progress and growth.

The importance of logical reasoning for society cannot be overstated. It facilitates rational decision-making, enhances critical thinking skills, and fosters problem-solving abilities. By cultivating logical thinking and reasoning in everyday life, individuals can contribute to a more informed, efficient, and democratic society. Whether it is in personal relationships, professional endeavors, or civic engagement, logical reasoning empowers individuals to navigate the complexities of life with clarity and confidence. Therefore, it is crucial for society to recognize and prioritize the cultivation of logical thinking, as it holds the key to a brighter and more prosperous future for all.

WHY LOGICAL THINKING IS NOT A PRIORITY IN TODAY'S SOCIETY

In our information-driven society, logical thinking seems to have taken a back seat to instant gratification, emotional responses, and social media influence. As a result, critical reasoning and logical analysis are not given the priority they deserve. This subchapter aims to shed light on why logical thinking is not a priority in today's society.

One of the primary reasons for this shift is the rise of social media and its impact on our lives. With the constant influx of information and the need to stay connected, people tend to focus more on quick reactions and opinions rather than logical reasoning. The need to have an immediate response, often driven by emotional triggers, outweighs the importance of thoughtful analysis.

The education system also plays a significant role in diminishing the importance of logical thinking. Many educational institutions emphasize rote learning and exam-oriented teaching methods, leaving little room for nurturing critical thinking skills. Students are seldom encouraged to question, analyze, or seek logical explanations. As a result, they grow up without developing the necessary skills to apply logical thinking in everyday situations.

Another contributing factor is the overwhelming influence of advertising and marketing. Companies typically use emotional appeals to manipulate consumer decisions, diverting attention from logical reasoning. Advertisements are designed to evoke emotions and create associations, leading individuals to make impulsive choices rather than considering the logical consequences of their actions.

The fast-paced nature of our society promotes instant gratification, discouraging people from investing time and effort in logical analysis. The desire for quick fixes and immediate results takes precedence over the meticulous process of logical thinking. As a result, people often overlook the long-term benefits and fail to consider the potential risks or consequences of their actions.

However, it is crucial to recognize the significance of logical thinking and reasoning in everyday life. Logical thinking helps individuals make informed decisions, solve problems effectively, and navigate complex situations. It enables us to analyze information critically, identify fallacies, and separate facts from opinions. By prioritizing logical thinking, society can make better choices, promote rational discourse, and foster a more informed and balanced community. Logical thinking is not given the priority it deserves in today's society due to the influence of social media, shortcomings in the education system, manipulative marketing techniques, and the desire for instant gratification. However, society can strive towards a more thoughtful and rational approach in everyday life by acknowledging the importance of logical thinking and nurturing critical reasoning skills.

FINAL THOUGHTS AND ENCOURAGEMENT FOR UNLOCKING YOUR FULL POTENTIAL

Congratulations! By embarking on this journey to develop your logical thinking skills, you have taken a significant step towards unlocking your full potential. Throughout this book, we have explored the power of logical thinking and how it can positively impact various aspects of your life. As we conclude, let us reflect on some final thoughts and provide you with the encouragement you need to continue on this path.

To businessmen/women, logical thinking is an invaluable asset in making informed decisions, solving complex problems, and fostering innovation. Remember that every setback is an opportunity to learn and grow. Trust your logical instincts and apply them to navigate the challenges that lie ahead.

Embrace logical reasoning to drive your businesses towards success.

To the mothers, logical thinking offers a framework for effective parenting and decision-making. Trust your logical intuition in raising your children, making choices for their education, and managing your household. Remember, logical thinking can help you strike a balance between your personal and family life, empowering you to be the best version of yourself.

To the students, logical thinking is the key to academic excellence. Develop your critical thinking skills, question assumptions, and seek evidence-based answers. Embrace the power of logical reasoning in your studies, enabling you to excel in exams, projects, and future careers. Remember, logical thinking is a lifelong skill that transcends the classroom.

To the workers, logical thinking empowers you to navigate the complexities of the workplace. Use logical reasoning to analyze problems, identify solutions, and communicate your ideas effectively.

Embrace the power of logical thinking to accelerate your professional growth and achieve your career goals.

To the Public servants, logical thinking provides a solid foundation for effective governance and decision-making. Let logical reasoning guide your policies, enabling you to make fair and well-informed choices that benefit society as a whole. Embrace the power of logical thinking to create positive change and build a better future for your constituents.

To the athletes, logical thinking can enhance your performance both on and off the field. Apply logical reasoning to strategize, analyze your opponents, and overcome obstacles. Embrace the power of logical thinking to unlock your full athletic potential, enabling you to achieve greatness in your chosen sport.

Logical thinking knows no bounds. It is a skill that can transform your personal and professional life. As you continue on this journey, remember to trust your logical instincts, embrace challenges as opportunities for growth, and apply logical reasoning in every aspect of your life. Unlock your full potential and let logical thinking be your guiding light towards a brighter and more successful future.

Thank you for taking the time to read my book. I have tested all of these techniques in the book. I hope you find them useful. Remember to look for my other books available at all the book retailers.

— *Kevin*

www.ingramcontent.com/pod-product-compliance
Lightning Source LLC
Chambersburg PA
CBHW061305120726
48001CB00001B/481